MASTER
YOUR SHORT
GAME
IN 16 DAYS

Also by the authors

Break 100 in 21 Days: A How-to Guide for the Weekend Golfer
Correct the 10 Most Common Golf Problems in 10 Days
Two-Putt Greens in 18 Days: A How-to Guide for the Weekend Golfer
Power Swing in 15 Days: A How-to Guide for the Weekend Golfer

MASTER YOUR SHORT GAME IN 16 DAYS

A How-to Guide for the Weekend Golfer

WALTER OSTROSKE
PGA Teaching Pro

and JOHN DEVANEY

Photography by Aime J. LaMontagne

A PERIGEE BOOK

Perigee Books
are published by
The Berkley Publishing Group
200 Madison Avenue
New York, NY 10016

Library of Congress Cataloging-in-Publication Data

Ostroske, Walter.
    Master your short game in 16 days : a how-to guide for the weekend
  golfer / Walter Ostroske and John Devaney : photographs by Aime J.
  LaMontagne.
        p.   cm.
    "A Perigee Book."
    ISBN 0-399-51861-4
    1. Short game (Golf)   I. Devaney, John.   II. Title.
  GV979.S54088   1993   93-36213 CIP
  796.352′3—dc20

Cover design by Richard Rossiter
Cover photograph by Aime J. LaMontagne

Printed in the United States of America
1 2 3 4 5 6 7 8 9 10

This book is printed on acid-free paper.
∞

To my longtime friend Bob Dempsey

—W.O.

Contents

Why Your Short Game Can Be Your Scoring Game

You probably have heard this complaint from other golfers:

"I don't know why I am not scoring lower," the golfer grouses. "I am hitting a lot longer off the tee. I am hitting longer off the fairway by ten to fifteen yards. I'm putting better. But I still can't break a hundred!" Or "I still can't break ninety." Or "I somehow can't break eighty."

When I hear these wails, I ask the golfer: "How's your short game?"

My fellow PGA professionals—both teaching pros and touring pros—call the short game The Scoring Game. You may drive a ball off a tee 225 yards—but you may face some 225 more yards to the green. That's two more swings. If one swing sends the ball hooking or slicing, you'll pay the penalty by adding at least two extra strokes to hole out.

But suppose you hit only a mediocre 190-yard drive. Suppose you then hit only a mediocre 160-yard second shot with a fairway wood. Now you stand within 100 yards of the green. You take out your pitching wedge and pitch that ball to within 5 feet of the pin. You ram home the putt. With three ordinary shots and one great one—your short-game shot—you got a

Walter Ostroske: "The short game is the Great Equalizer."

par. Do that on two or three holes during a round and you will almost certainly break the 100, 90 or whatever barrier you have been yearning to break.

Like putting, the short game is The Great Equalizer. When you putt you are the equal of Jack Nicklaus or Fred Couples or Ray Floyd: They can make a 20-foot putt, but so can you. In fact, so can a ten-year-old child. You can't hit drives or long fairway shots with the distance and accuracy of Couples, but you sure can knock in a ten-footer just as he does. And just like Nicklaus, Couples or Floyd, you can hit a ball 100 yards. Anyone can hit a ball 100 yards, including that ten-year-old child.

But while putting and the short game are both The Great Equalizers, I tell weekenders that you can shave strokes more quickly off your handicap—go from a 30 handicap to a 25 handicap, for example—by mastering your short game first, *then* polishing your putting game. Here's why:

Luck has a lot to do with great putting on any one round. I tell golfers that I can control a putt—its speed and its direction—for only the first 6 feet that it rolls across the carpet. Then other fingers begin to steer the ball: the slope of the green, the thickness of the grass, bumps and spike holes. I can only hope that the luck of the green will bring that ball close to where I aimed.

But when I go to my short game to pitch or chip, I loft the ball into the air where there are no bumps or slopes. True, there might be wind, but I can use the wind to help carry or blow the ball onto the green. And when a pitch or chip shot bounces onto a green, each bounce upward is much more likely to go straight than a putt curling across a slanted green.

Luck is always a factor in golf. But luck counts less in the short game than it does in putting. What counts most in the short game is skill, specifically what we call *touch and feel.* If you can hone those two skills, touch and feel, they will do more for shaving strokes off your score than any other skill in golf, including hitting drives as far as John Daly.

In fact, I have seen this happen so often I no longer think it unusual: A long hitter and a short hitter play a round. On a long par-5 hole, the long hitter stands within 100 yards of the green after two shots. But he lands short of the green with his approach, finally gets on in four, then two-putts for a bogey six.

The short hitter needs three strokes to get within 50 yards of the green. But from there he rifles a pitch that stops close enough to the pin for a one-putt and a par-5.

Like that long hitter off the tee, most weekenders hit their approach shots short of the green. Why?

They make at least three mistakes so obvious that I am sure I can erase them from your short game within a few days. Let's begin by going to Day One and checking out the short-game clubs, the short-game grip, the short-game setup and the basic bread-and-butter short-game swing.

The Short-Game Swing: It Needs No Help

What is more frustrating (in a game often filled with frustrations) than to whack a ball off a tee some 220 yards, hit a three-wood another 190 yards, stand only 70 yards from a par-5 green with an excellent chance for a birdie or par—and hit your approach shot short?

You have wasted a stroke. Now, from, say, 10 yards away, you must hit another approach shot to get on the green in four strokes instead of three. After having come all that distance with two superb shots, you have wasted both with a weak approach.

Why do nearly all high-handicappers hit their approach shots short of the green? Most make at least one of these three mistakes:

1. They hit the ball on their upswing. They shift their weight forward, like a boxer throwing a punch, and try to "pick up" or scoop up the ball the way you might use a child's toy shovel to flip a ball up out of a sandbox. By hitting the ball on the upswing, the golfer gets plenty of height—but not enough distance.

By shifting their weight forward with their approach shots, weekenders make the mistake of scooping the ball—and landing it short.

2. They set up incorrectly, placing the ball so that it's closer to the front foot than the rear foot. Almost inevitably, they impact the ball on the upswing.

3. On the downswing, the golfer says to himself, "Uh-oh, I'm swinging too fast and I'll hit the ball over the green." So the golfer slows down the swing, decelerating just before impact. The short-game swing becomes a weak swing—weak at impact and weak during the follow-through. The golfer thinks that because the distance is short, the swing should be slow.

Yet the reverse is true: The shorter the distance, the faster the swing should be.

Let me explain: When you stand at a tee and want to hit a ball 200 yards, you choose a driver or some other long-shafted club. The long shaft and big clubhead are made to give you distance. You don't have to swing at 100 miles an hour to drive the ball 200 yards. You know that if you swing at 50 miles an hour, you will get those 200 yards—while reducing considerably your chances for a mis-hit.

When you are aiming at a green from, say, 50 yards away, however, you choose a short iron. These clubs have the shortest shafts in your bag. That means they will trace a much smaller swing arc than the arc traced by a driver. And the smaller the arc, the slower the clubhead speed at impact. The slower the clubhead speed, the less distance you are going to get.

What's more, these short-game clubs have faces with the highest lofts of any clubs in your bag. Their faces are built to give you height, not distance.

The short iron, held in my right hand, will trace a shorter swing arc than the driver in my left hand.

What this means to your swing: To get the distance you need, *you must impact the ball with a more forceful swing than you would use when swinging the longer-shafted clubs.*

Let's take a closer look at that short-game swing, starting with the grip.

THE GRIP

Grip the short irons as you grip any other club, with this exception: Apply a little less finger pressure on the shaft but apply a little more pressure with both

Grip the short iron as you grip any other club—but with a little more pressure with the thumbs.

The clubface, when turned in, will cause a hook.

The clubface, when turned out, will cause a slice.

thumbs. Make sure the clubface meets the ball square to the target. By applying a little less finger pressure— say, 35 pounds (to pick a number) instead of 50—and a little more thumb pressure, you are helping to ensure that the toe of the clubface doesn't turn in (causing a hook) or out (causing a slice).

When you hit with the longer clubs, you can hook a little or slice a little and still land on a fairway no more than 20 or 30 yards off target. Land 20 or 30 yards off the green with a short iron and you have wasted a stroke.

The important thing about the short-game grip is that you want your hands to feel comfortably loose and free. This is a hands-and-arms-and-shoulders swing. And it is through the hands that we give what we call *touch and feel* to the clubhead as it sends the ball to the pin.

THE SETUP

Two important things to remember:

1. Place the ball in the middle of your stance or an inch or 2 toward your rear foot. Placing the ball toward your front foot will cause you to contact the ball on the upswing, hitting high but short. By placing the ball in the middle of your stance or a shade toward your rear foot, you will strike the ball on the downswing. You first hit the ball and then continue downward so the club slides into the turf, digging a divot and helping to create backspin.

2. Your weight should be mostly on the back of your heels, not on the soles or on your toes. Assume a slight

The short iron contacts the ball, placed near the middle of the stance, on the downswing, then slices into the turf, digging a divot.

An open stance opens up room on the front side for arms and hands to swing past the body.

Stand far enough away so that a ball dropped from the chin would hit the ball on the ground.

sitting position so that the clubhead, with its shorter shaft, can reach the bottom of the ball and the turf during the downswing.

I recommend a square stance, with your toes at right angles to a line that is parallel to the target line. But some golfers feel more comfortable with the short-shafted clubs when they open their stance, moving their front foot a couple of inches back from the parallel line. That opens up room on their front side for their arms and hands to swing the club past the body after impact. Whether you use a square or a slightly open stance is up to you and how comfortable you feel in your stance.

How far do you stand from the ball? I stand so that my head, nose and chin are over the ball. Drop a ball from my chin and it will hit the ball at my feet. I feel that my arms and hands have the space to move freely during the upswing, the downswing and the through swing. I do not feel that my arms are overextended, nor do I feel that my arms are in a crowded space. In short, I am saying that you should stand in what I call your "comfort zone."

If you are tall and thin, you will likely stand closer to the ball than a golfer who is shorter and thicker around the middle. He or she will need to stand back a little to allow space for the arms to get around the tummy.

THE SWING

Look at the sequence photos on the following pages showing my swing with a short iron. You will see first of all that it is a swing made only with the arms, hands and shoulders. You can also see that on both the takeaway and the follow-through, I bring up my hands to shoulder level. This is what we pros call a balanced swing—the ends must match up.

Second, you will see that my body does not move until after I have impacted the ball. My chest, hips, knees and feet come around—just as they would for a swing with a longer-shafted club—*but only a half-second or so after impact.* It's like a one-two punch:

One, the hands, arms and shoulders come through, leading the parade; two, the body shifts its weight

The swing with a short iron is a swing only with the arms, hands and shoulders.

Since I brought up my hands to the shoulders on the takeaway, I brought up my hands to the shoulders on the follow-through. The ends must match up.

The body comes around only well after impact. That ensures that the clubhead will point to the target during the follow-through.

from the back foot to the front foot and follows the clubhead at the end of the parade.

Why is there a delay in the weight shift during the short-iron swing? Because we don't need a lot of distance. Hence we don't need to throw the weight of the body behind the swing. *The body stays out of the action until after the event*—that is, when the ball is already on its way to the target. The body then comes around to ensure that the clubhead points to the target during the follow-through, giving us accuracy.

Trouble is, we are all used to shifting our weight to the front side before impact. That's the key, we have been told, to gobbling up lots of distance. And we have been told correctly, but it does not apply to the short game. Now we don't need lots of distance. We need, most of all, accuracy in length and accuracy in direction.

So the body must stay out of the swing until after impact. But golfers move the body before impact out of habit, as I have just mentioned, or because they are trying to help the shot by scooping up the ball. The short-game swing doesn't need help. All it needs is a slow takeaway, a firm but not overly fast downswing, crisp contact between the lofted clubface and the bottom of the ball and a follow-through that matches the takeaway in pace and rhythm and length. Then, as the arms and hands go past the body, the body comes around.

That's your bread-and-butter short-game swing, the one you will use with all the short-game clubs (see box on page 30). But as we will see during the next week or so, the way you swing from 100 yards out is not the way you swing from 10 yards out—or from a bad lie.

To keep body movement out of the swing, practice swinging with the feet and legs close together.

TOUCH-AND-FEEL DRILLS

1. This drill encourages you to swing with only the hands, arms and shoulders, eliminating body movement and taking the lower gear—hips, knees and feet—out of the action. Stand in front of a mirror with a short club in your hands. Keep your feet and legs close together. Swing with only your hands, arms and shoulders at an imaginary ball while watching yourself in the mirror. Your belt buckle should not move. Do that for 15 minutes.

Again stand with your feet and legs close together, this time at a range or in your backyard. Swing at a real or plastic ball with only your hands, arms and shoulders. By keeping your feet close together, you eliminate the lower gear from the swing, keeping your body out of the action and encouraging a swing that is made faster at impact by the hands and arms—not by the body.

2. This next drill encourages you to make the ends of your swing match up in distance and in pace and rhythm. Take your swing back so that your hands reach waist high. Bring the club down and impact a ball—it doesn't matter where the ball goes—and then follow through until your hands reach waist high. Do that for 10 minutes. Then make a swing so that your hands reach shoulder high on both the backswing and the through swing; again it does not matter where the ball goes. Do that for 10 minutes. Then swing so your hands reach knee high on both the backswing and the through swing. Do that for 10 minutes.

The Short-Game Clubs

They are the seven-iron, eight-iron, nine-iron, the pitching wedge, the sand wedge (with its wide flange for blasting) and the L wedge. Many pros (I am one of them) carry a sand wedge with a lot of loft on the clubface but with a very small and narrow flange. I use it when I need quick loft and a quick stop—for example, when I am pitching over a mound to a nearby pin.

The pitching wedge differs from the normal sand wedge in that the pitching wedge gives you twice the distance you get from a sand wedge when hitting from grass or rough. But the pitching wedge won't get the ball up as quickly or as high as the sand wedge. And the thick flange on the sand wedge can dig deeper into sand to get the ball to rise on a cloud of sand.

The L wedge has a severe amount of loft to lob the ball over obstacles and a face that imparts a great deal of spin for a quick stop.

The short-game clubs, left to right: the nine-iron, the pitching wedge, the sand wedge, the L wedge.

Touch and Feel: The Great Intangibles

You are Lee Trevino or Nick Faldo or Curtis Strange and you are pitching to a green. You pick your club, probably a pitching wedge. You stand over the ball. You know that you are within 70 yards of the green, and the hole is cut about 30 feet away from the front of the green. You figure you need to pitch the ball 77 yards and 2 feet to drop the ball into the hole for an eagle two.

You stand over the ball. You bring back the club to hip height—your height for a shot of 77 yards and 2 feet. You bring down the club to impact at a certain speed—your speed for a shot of 77 yards and 2 feet. You bring up the club in the through swing to hip height—your height for a shot of 77 yards and 2 feet.

The ball flies straight to the pin and stops 1 foot short of the pin. You drop in the putt for your birdie three.

True, the ball did not travel 77 yards and 2 feet. It traveled 77 yards and 1 foot. Most touring pros will settle for a short-game tolerance error of 1 foot.

So would you.

You would settle, in fact, for a tolerance error of 5 yards—5 yards short or 5 yards long.

You can be that accurate, I assure you, if you:

1. Understand what I mean by *touch and feel.*

2. Hit at least 20 golf balls each day during the next four weeks while practicing the drills that I will give you. Practice those drills at the end of each day's lesson for the next 14 days.

WHAT IS TOUCH AND FEEL?

A golfer has touch and feel when he or she hits a ball with a short iron and feels, through the touching of the hands on the grip, that the ball will go the distance the golfer aimed for—or that it is going to land short or long. The golfer doesn't have to look at the ball's flight. Touch and feel tells the golfer, without raising his or her head, that the ball is going to go the distance the golfer has programmed the ball to go—or (if he or she has programmed it wrong) that the ball is going to go short or long.

Golfers can gauge how far the ball will go by deciding (1) how far they will bring the club away from the target on the upswing, (2) how slow or fast they will bring down the club to impact the ball, and (3) how far they will bring the club toward the target on the through swing.

Let's be even more specific. Let's look at my swing with a short iron. I know—as you will see during tomorrow's lesson—that if (1) I bring my hands up to my shoulders on the backswing, and that if (2) I bring the clubhead down at a certain speed (let's say 50 miles an hour), and if (3) I bring my hands up to my shoulders—matching the ends—in the through swing, the ball should go exactly 100 yards, give or take 5 yards.

That doesn't mean *you* can pitch a ball exactly 100 yards if you bring your hands to the shoulders on the backswing and to the shoulders on the through swing while you impact the ball at the exact speed with which I impacted the ball. That's because we are all built differently, with different arm and hand strengths, and different eye-hand-ball coordination skills, to name just a few differences.

To sum up: You may need to bring your hands higher or lower and you may need to swing faster or slower to pitch a ball exactly 100 yards.

How do you find out what your swing distance and clubhead speed should be for a shot of 100 yards? Determine your own personal "gauge" for a 100-yard shot by looking at the diagram on the next page. This diagram shows my own swing distance and clubhead speed for a shot of 70 yards. For every distance, paced off in 5-yard increments, I own a different gauge— and so can you.

Your 50-yard gauge, for example, may tell you that if you: (1) bring your hands up so they are exactly even with, say, your kneecaps on the upswing, and (2) bring down the clubhead at a speed a little faster than you bring down the clubhead for a shot of 40 yards (say, at 50 miles an hour instead of 40 miles an hour), and (3) match the ends with a through swing that finishes with your hands at the kneecaps, the ball will go 50 yards.

Golfers ask me, "Where do you buy gauges like that, Walter? I'll give you a blank check for a dozen of them."

"You *can* buy them," I answer. "And they'll cost you nothing in dollars. But they will cost you time—lots of practice time. You must go to a range or to a backyard

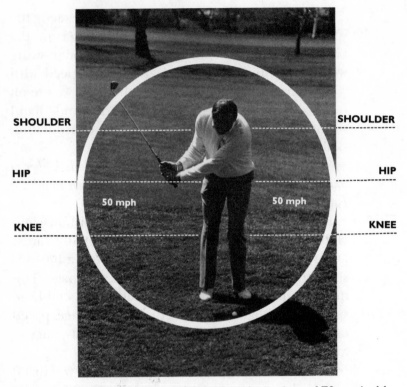

This is my personal touch and feel gauge for a shot of 70 yards. My hands go as high as my hips on the downswing and the through swing. I bring the club down and through at 50 mph. Your own personal touch and feel gauge may tell you that for a shot of this distance, you need to bring your hands higher and that you must bring down the clubhead faster.

and hit a lot of balls. Through trial and error, you find how far a ball will go with a certain swing arc and with a certain swing speed."

I also tell golfers: "When we say that touch and feel is something we can't see (or even touch!), it may be difficult to understand. But suppose I asked you to toss a ball so it would land ten yards away—no more, no less. You would hold the ball in your hand, swing the hand back, then swing it forward and toss the ball gently, your hand probably dropping no lower than waist level. If I asked you to throw another ball thirty yards, no more and no less, you would swing your hand back perhaps to near shoulder level. And you would bring your hand forward much faster than you brought it forward for the toss of ten yards. And, finally, you would swing your hand much lower, perhaps to your knees, to add 'send' to the ball.

"It's the same thing in golf."

Then I add this: "You would grip the ball lightly for a short toss, grip it more tightly to throw it a long way. Same thing in golf. You grip the longer clubs with more finger pressure, as I said yesterday, than you grip the shorter clubs. If you choke the short irons too tightly, the swing will be herky-jerky and less fluid, for one thing, and a choking grip can choke off the feel of the ball against the clubhead at impact."

Now, if you understand that, you are ready for the first of my touch-and-feel drills. I offer these two incentives for working as hard as possible during the next month or longer at these touch-and-feel drills:

1. Whether you are a tour player or a beginner, you will never be a consistently good golfer if your short game lacks touch and feel.

2. More golf tournaments and matches have been won by touch and feel than by drives of 350 yards.

TOUCH-AND-FEEL DRILLS

1. Set a marker exactly 50 yards from where you stand. Pace out the yardage yourself, one long stride being one yard. If you are not sure you can pace the yardage correctly, find an empty football field that has yardage markers.

Swing at a ball, aiming to hit it at least 20 yards beyond the marker. Hit five balls beyond the marker. Then shorten the arc of your swing and slow down your speed so that you finally make one ball stop within 5 yards of the marker.

Now you want to instill into your muscle memory the swing arc and swing speed you used to hit that ball 50 yards. Keep hitting golf balls until you make five balls in a row stop within 5 yards of that 50-yard marker.

2. Hold a short-iron club with the last three fingers of the left hand and the left thumb. Keep the first finger off. Place the right thumb and first finger on the grip. Keep the other fingers of the right hand off the club. Swing the club slowly five times, making an upswing, a downswing and a through swing. You will get the feeling of having full support of the club even though you are not fully gripping the club. Then grip the club as you normally do and make five full swings. Swing the club with both grips for 15 minutes. This will teach you that even with only about half your fingers on the club, you are supporting the club as firmly as if you had all your fingers on the grip. There is no need to squeeze or choke the club.

DAY THREE _____

The Short-Game Swing from 100 Yards Out

I said earlier that we all can hit a golf ball 100 yards. Yet a distance the length of a football field is a distance to be respected. You certainly won't cover that distance with a ho-hum lazy-man's swing. From this distance— or from any distance beyond 100 yards—the golfer must keep two aspects of the swing very much foremost in the mind:

1. I need impact.

2. I need send.

I NEED IMPACT

For a solid impact that will get me the distance I need, I must position the clubhead correctly on the up- swing. That means bringing the club *up*. I repeat: *UP*.

Too many golfers, especially from this distance, bring the club back and *around*. As the photos on the following pages show, you should bring the club up so that the clubhead points to the target. You should not bring the clubhead around, the way a baseball hitter cocks his bat. If you bring the clubhead around, you will bring the clubhead down and around, impacting

37

RIGHT! You bring the club up so that the clubhead is pointing toward the target.

WRONG! Bringing the club up and around will bring the club down and around, impacting the ball with a glancing blow.

The belt buckle stays opposite the ball until after impact.

the ball with a glancing blow. The result is a hook or a slice that will very likely send the ball into a greenside bunker on the left or right.

I end my upswing with my hands where I know they should be positioned for this distance from my touch-and-feel drills. I bring the clubhead down while keeping my body facing the ball. My belt buckle will be directly opposite the ball until after impact.

I strike the ball with a downward blow. One of the oldest axioms in golf is that you must hit down to get the ball up. You sweep a ball off a tee with a driver, but a ball on a tee is already in the air. To send a ball lying on the fairway turf up into the air, you must hit down so that you contact the bottom of the ball.

The force of your swing will continue downward. That means, of necessity, that your clubhead carves a path through the turf—the well-known divot. What's important now is that the impact of the clubhead contacting the ball and turf does not—I repeat, *does not*—slow down your clubhead because . . .

I NEED SEND

For a shot of this distance, it is especially important that the through swing be completed with as full and high an arc as the backswing. The ends must match! If you took the clubhead back on the upswing so that your hands came to shoulder height, as mine are doing in these photos, the hands must again reach as high as the shoulders at the end of the through swing.

For all short-game swings, it's important that the follow-through be as extended as the upswing. If you quit on the through swing, the clubhead will not point

On shots of this distance, it is especially important that the ends match. If the hands reach shoulder high on the backswing, they must reach shoulder high on the through swing.

toward the target at the "shaking hands" position. The clubhead will tend to point left or right, causing the ball to go left or right.

A ball that flies left or right of your target is bad enough. But if you quit after impact for a shot of this distance, you will not add enough force to the shot. Or, as I like to say, you are taking away the "send." The ball will not only drop left or right, it will also drop short.

Today, so far, I have stressed that sending a ball 100 or more yards to a green is a distance that demands respect. You can't take a lah-de-dah swing.

But—and I am also stressing this—*you must keep your body out of this swing just as you would for a swing of half this distance. This is strictly a swing for your shoulders, arms and hands, whether you are sending the ball 100 yards or 10 yards.* The lower gear—hips, knees and feet— must stay still until after impact. There will be no shifting of the weight from the back foot to the front foot until after impact. As in all short-game swings, the big muscles of the body stay out of the action.

When should weight shift take place?

My answer: The clubhead must bring the lower gear and the body around *after the clubhead has impacted the ball and sent it on its way.*

The next questions are obvious: How long must the lower gear and the body stay still? When do they come around?

My answer is this: The timing varies, depending on the length of the shot. The longer the shot, the quicker the lower gear and the body must come around to add "send" to the shot.

For a shot of 100 yards or more with the pitching

If you quit on the through swing, the clubhead will point left or right of the target, causing the ball to go left or right.

wedge, eight-iron or nine-iron, the belt buckle and the feet must stay pointed toward the ball until after the clubhead passes the front leg. For shots of shorter distances, as we will see tomorrow, the weight shift takes place later in the follow-through.

TOUCH-AND-FEEL DRILLS

1. Set out markers at 100 and 125 yards. Hit a dozen balls in a row that land within 10 yards of the 125-yard marker. If one ball lands more than 10 yards away from the marker, start over again until you have planted 12 in a row within 10 yards of the marker. Now hit a dozen balls in a row that land within 5 yards of the 100-yard marker. Estimate how many inches you took away from the arc for the swing of 125 yards to make the swing that landed close to the 100-yard marker. Also estimate how much speed you used for the downswing for 100 yards compared to the downswing for 125 yards. Now make your own personal touch-and-feel gauge for 100 yards, similar to mine (for 70 yards) shown on page 34.

2. Swing the club with both feet and legs together for 15 minutes, forcing yourself to keep your legs and body out of the action. Then move your feet and legs apart and swing, but again keep your belt buckle facing straight ahead toward where the ball would be, using only your feet and legs for balance. Do that for 15 minutes. You will be instilling in your muscle memory the feeling of keeping your body out of the action until well after impact.

From 75 Yards Out

Yesterday, when hitting from 100 yards away, I instructed you to bring your hands to shoulder level on the upswing while swinging a pitching wedge. Today we are 25 yards closer to the green. But again we'll swing a pitching wedge. By choosing the same club for pitching from these distances, we feed consistent information to our touch-and-feel gauge, which tells us the length of our swing arc and the speed of the downward blow.

Let's see how this works for a pitch of 75 yards. I bring up the hands to slightly below shoulder level. To be more specific, I bring up the hands to 3 inches below the point where I brought them up for the 100-yard shot. I bring down the club at a speed that is about 10 percent slower than the speed I brought it down for the 100-yard shot. And I follow through so that my hands rise to just below shoulder level—3 inches below the point where I brought them up for the 100-yard shot.

I have taken 6 inches off my swing arc: 3 inches off the backswing, 3 inches off the through swing. After hitting hundreds of balls in practice, I have found—and my personal touch-and-feel gauge confirms this—that a swing arc 6 inches shorter gives me a shot that travels 75 yards, give or take maybe a couple of yards.

Now let's be clear about this: That doesn't mean that if *you* take 6 inches off *your* 100-yard swing arc and impact the ball with 10 percent less clubhead speed you will hit a ball exactly 75 yards.

Your own personal touch-and-feel gauge must tell you, after hitting balls for the drills I will be giving you each day, exactly how long your swing arc should be for a shot of 75 yards and exactly how fast you should bring down the clubhead to send the ball 75 yards.

But two things can be said with certainty: The closer you get to the green, the shorter your swing arc will be and the slower your swing speed will be.

One other thing will change as the distance to the green shrinks. You will continue to take a divot, of course, since you are still making a downward blow. But because the speed of the downswing becomes slower, the clubhead has less force as it digs into the turf. The divot will be shorter and shallower for a shot of 75 yards than for a shot of 100 yards.

Finally, the weight shift occurs a little later than it does for the 100-yard shot. Your body and the belt buckle should come around *after* the clubhead has passed your left leg and is beginning its upward arc.

TOUCH-AND-FEEL DRILLS

1. Set a marker at 100 yards and another at 75 yards. Hit a dozen balls in a row that travel to the 100-yard marker or no more than 10 yards past it. Then hit five balls in a row that land within 5 yards of the 75-yard marker. Write down your estimate of how many inches you took off the swing arc for the 75-yard shots

Standing on your left or right foot, swing at an imaginary ball.
The drill will teach you to use only the arms.

compared to the 100-yard shots. If you brought up the hands 2 inches below the level for the 100-yard pitch and finished your through swing with your hands 2 inches below the level for 100 yards, you took 4 inches off your swing arc. Also write down how fast you brought down the clubhead, giving the speed for the 100-yard shots an arbitrary number of 50 miles an hour. If your touch and feel tells you that you brought down the clubhead about 10 percent slower than you did for the 100-yard shot, your speed for the 75-yard shot would be 45 miles an hour. Thus your gauge for 75-yard shots should show 45-mile-an-hour clubhead speed and a swing arc 4 inches shorter than the arc for 100-yard shots.

2. Stand on your left foot, grip a pitching wedge and swing at an imaginary ball. If you topple, start over until you make five straight swings while standing on the one foot. Then, standing on your right foot, make five straight swings without losing your balance. This drill will teach you a steady, controlled swing using only your arms.

From Within 55 Yards of the Green

Up to now we have been talking about shooting for the green. Now, from 55 yards, we are aiming for the pin or, at the very least, for the section of the green where the pin is located.

When you stand this close, it is vital that you know the exact yardage you must cover to the pin. Course markers—metal plates in the turf or distances marked on sprinkler heads—tell you that from the marker to the green is 100 yards, 75 yards or 50 yards. You can then pace off the distance from the marker to your ball—one long stride equals one yard—to determine how far you stand from the front of the green. From this distance you should be able to see how far the pin is from the front of the green. If your ball is 23 yards, or paces, past the 75-yard marker, you need to cover 52 yards to the green. And if the pin is cut 30 feet away from the green's front, you need to cover 62 yards to land next to the pin.

I can't stress enough how important it is to know your exact yardage when you get this close to the green. From 100 yards away our tolerance for error could be 10 yards, and we will still land on the green with a chance to two-putt. But as we move within 55 yards of the green, the tolerance for error should be about 5 yards or less because now we are looking to one-putt that green.

My feet are set about shoulder-width apart. I shorten my grip on the pitching wedge, bringing my hands down about halfway on the grip. I make sure that most of my weight is on the back of my heels. Since I have shortened my grip, I must bend a little more at the knees, "sitting down" a little more than I did from 75 or 100 yards. I want to make sure that I contact the bottom half of the ball with the clubhead at address and at impact.

The takeaway is slow and unhurried. It is lazy in its rhythm. It is the takeaway that is the undoing of many weekenders when they swing from this distance. They bring the clubhead up and *back*, not up and *up*. They think they need a shallow arc for a shot of this distance. They're wrong! They need a steep arc for a distance of 55 yards, just as they need a steep arc for any short-game swing. It is the steep arc that creates the descending blow—hitting down, as we have been saying, to get the ball up.

When golfers hit the ball with that shallow arc, they are likely to hit the ball at its equator, often producing a low line drive that hits the ground 20 or 30 yards away, bounces off the target line and rolls to a stop well short of the green.

Remember: The takeaway is an up-*up* move—not an up-and-back move.

Your hands come up to wherever your touch-and-feel gauge tells you is the right point—in my case, a little above the knees. That point, of course, is below where I would bring my hands up for a shot of 75 yards.

Result: a shorter downswing arc. A shorter swing arc means slower clubhead speed at impact. That's good, since we don't want to drive the ball over the green, but we don't want the speed to be so slow that we drop the ball short of the green.

Your shoulders, arms and hands, therefore, must bring down the clubhead with enthusiasm and with crispness (while you keep the rest of your body out of the action). The shorter arc produces slower clubhead speed, so leave that job to the smaller arc; you should impact the ball with all the clubhead speed you can muster.

Your shoulders, arms and hands must follow through with the same enthusiasm, breaking the surface of the turf with the divot. On the through swing, of course, bring your hands to that exact point— knees or wherever—that they reached on the take-away.

Finally, when the clubhead is just beginning its upward arc on the through swing, your body—from your feet to your eyebrows—follows the clubhead around, helping to guarantee that you are keeping the clubhead pointing straight at the pin. You will note again, I hope, that the shorter the distance to the green, the longer the delay in bringing your body around after the clubhead. Put another way: the shorter the distance, the bigger the gap between your belt buckle and the clubhead during the follow-through swing.

Feet are shoulder width, hands are about halfway down the grip, weight is on the back of my heels, and I bend a little more at the knees.

TOUCH-AND-FEEL DRILLS

1. Take a stronger club than you would use for this distance (within 55 yards of the green). With a nine-iron or even an eight-iron, use the same swing arc and the same swing speed that you would use with a pitching wedge. Swing at five balls. All five should go beyond your target. Now take a pitching wedge or whatever club you like for this distance. Swing with the same arc and the same speed. The ball should go about 55 yards, give or take 5 yards. Alternating between the stronger club and the club you like for this distance, hit 50 balls. This will help you relate the swing's touch and feel to the yardage you need to cover.

2. Repeat the first drill for Day One, keeping your legs and feet close together and swinging at plastic or real balls for half an hour. This drill again reminds your muscle memory to keep your body out of the swing until after impact.

DAY SIX

From 40 Yards Out

Again you are aiming for the pin or, at the very least, for that section of the green where the flag is fluttering. But from 40 yards or so, we come to a crossroad in deciding which club to swing.

Either the pitching wedge or the nine- or eight-iron will work here, depending on which is your comfort club for short-game shots. Or, from this short a distance, you can switch to the sand wedge.

Lots of golfers are surprised when I suggest the sand wedge for a shot from grass, but the sand wedge throws the ball a lot higher than the pitching wedge. From these distances you want the ball airborne during at least 90 percent of its journey, rolling no more than 10 percent of the distance. When you hit a ball with the sand wedge, the ball stops very quickly. What's more, the sand wedge's more lofted face reduces the danger of whacking the ball over the green. Its more lofted face gets the ball up—but it will soar only half the distance that you would get with the pitching wedge.

On the other hand, the pitching wedge has its own advantages over the sand wedge from this close a distance. The pitching wedge has a sharper flange. It cuts the turf surface a lot easier than the sand wedge's fatter flange, which might catch on the turf, stopping the clubhead before you can complete your through swing.

Then, too, the sand wedge can't dig a ball out of deep grass—not with that fat flange. In deep grass you need the cutting action of the pitching wedge. Moreover, if the grass is soggy or muddy, the thick flange of the sand wedge may get caught and slow down your clubhead speed. And, finally, the sand wedge is built for height, not distance. Asking it to propel a ball 40 yards is asking for its limit.

Which road do you take: sand wedge or pitching wedge? My answer is this: Choose the sand wedge only if the conditions are ideal. The ball should be propped up in a perfect lie on dry grass on a day with little or no wind. You don't want to hit the ball high with a sand wedge and leave it to the quirky mercies of a crosswind.

If the conditions are ideal for a sand wedge, I squeeze the grip a little more tightly with my fingers than I would with a pitching wedge. It is not a choking grip, but I want a firmer grip because I know the thick flange will catch on the grass before or after impact. I don't want the grass to twist the blade, turning the toe away from me (a slice) or toward me (a hook).

On the takeaway with the sand wedge, I bring my hands about shoulder high for a shot of this distance. I would bring them only to my waist if I were swinging a pitching wedge from this distance. I need the longer swing arc—and more clubhead speed—to cover the distance with a sand wedge. The reason: The sand wedge's higher degree of loft, as we've noted, is not built for distance. On the through swing I match the end by finishing with my hands shoulder high.

The body starts to come around only when the clubhead has passed above the knees.

But suppose I go the other road and choose the pitching wedge, the conditions not being ideal. I move my hands down on the grip, the fingers of my lower hand touching the metal shaft. By shortening my grip, I shorten the arc, since I need less clubhead speed for this distance.

On the takeaway I bring *my* hands *up* only waist high—*yours* will come to wherever your touch-and-feel gauge indicates. I bring down the club with as much force from my hands, arms and shoulders as I would use for longer distances. I know that the shorter swing arc will give me the clubhead speed I need for this distance.

I make a full follow-through, my hands reaching waist high. My body starts to come around only when the clubhead has climbed above the knees.

When you come to the crossroad at this distance or even closer to the green, and you must choose between the sand wedge and your most comfortable club, whether it be a pitching wedge or some other short iron, remember: Let the lie and other conditions tell you what to do.

Ideal conditions? Think sand wedge.

Less than ideal? Go with your most comfortable club.

TOUCH-AND-FEEL DRILLS

1. Take a club and hold it horizontally across your waist with your left hand. Grip another club with your right hand and bring it back to the height of the club in your left hand. Then, with no ball on the ground,

Bring the right-hand club down and through and up to the level of the club held level across your waist, knees or shoulders.

bring the right-hand club down and through and up to the level of the club held across your waist. Do that for 10 minutes. Then hold the horizontal club so that it is lower—between waist and knees—and again make a full swing arc, matching the ends. Do that for 10 minutes. Next hold the club so that it is level with your shoulders and again make a full swing arc with a club in your right hand. Do that for 10 minutes. This drill will teach your muscle memory the touch and feel of a swing arc that's equal on both sides.

Swing at the ball so that you shear the sheet of newspaper all the way through.

2. Tack a sheet of newspaper onto the grass in your backyard. Place a real or plastic ball in the middle of the sheet. Gripping a sand wedge, swing at the ball so that you shear the newspaper from the ball all the way through to the target side of the sheet. This will teach you the feeling of gripping the sand wedge extra firmly when you are hitting through grass or sand, helping to ensure that you keep the clubhead square to the target. Hit 10 balls off the newspaper, shearing the paper to its edge.

From 30 Yards Out

A short-iron shot from this distance is akin to a putt.
Now don't get me wrong. I don't mean you should
look to putt the ball from here, but the shot from
inside 30 yards is unique. For longer distances you
must make sure your clubhead is square to the target
line at impact and in the early portion of the through
swing. But now you must make sure your clubhead
stays square to the target line on the takeaway, on the
downswing, at impact and for much of the through
swing.

Sound familiar? Of course. That's exactly what you
do when you putt. You keep the putterhead square to
the target line from takeaway to follow-through.

You want to keep the clubhead square during most
of this swing of 30 yards or less for exactly the same
reason you want to keep the putter square all through
the putting stroke: You want the ball to go straight to
the cup.

From distances like 100 yards, you have the luxury
of knowing you don't need to hit a bull's-eye. If you hit
the ball 5 yards left or 5 yards right of your target from
100, 75 or even 40 yards away, that's just great. You are
on the green with a good-to-excellent chance of two-
putting.

But from this short distance, you want to shave
strokes off your game by one-putting. Why should you

You must keep the clubface of the short iron, held in my left hand, as square to the target line (shown by the clubshaft on the ground) as you would keep the head of a putter, held in my right hand, square to the target from takeaway to follow-through.

two-putt on a par-4 hole when you have hit a second
shot this close to the green? Your tolerance for error
has shrunk from 15 feet to 2 or 3 feet. That means it is
imperative that you hit the ball *straight* just as you putt
a ball straight.

To hit the ball straight, you can't allow the toe of the
clubhead—at impact or during the through swing—
to turn in (the ball will go left) or turn out (the ball
will go right). The clubhead must impact the ball so
that the clubface forms a right angle to the target line.

You also must be sure of your yardage to the pin.
Quickly pace off the yards from your ball to the pin
while someone else is taking a shot from the fairway.
When you know the exact yardage, your touch-and-
feel gauge will give you the length of your swing arc
and the speed of your downswing.

For this distance I shorten my grip so that the bottom three fingers of my lower hand are wrapped
around the metal of the shaft. I narrow my stance so
that my feet are inside my shoulders.

Some golfers like to use an open stance for this
short shot, drawing back their front foot from the
target line. They believe they get a more open look at
the flagstick. If an open stance makes you feel more
comfortable, then certainly take an open stance. But
whether you prefer an open stance or a square stance,
it is important that most of your weight be on the
backs of your heels. You will be "sitting down" more
than for the longer shots, since you are shortening
your grip on the club. You must "sit" lower to the ball.

I bring my hands up to about knee high with a slow,
unhurried upswing. I slow the takeaway by reminding

myself that I am close to the green and so there is no need to hurry to get there.

As I bring down the clubhead with my hands, arms and shoulders, I concentrate on:

1. making the clubhead square as soon as the downswing begins;

2. making a descending blow so that the clubhead impacts the bottom of the ball and continues downward through the turf, imparting *backspin.*

If I keep the clubhead square, the ball will go straight to the flag while it is airborne. But when it lands, I cannot control how straight it will roll. A spike mark could veer it left or right. Therefore, I want the ball to fly 95 percent of the distance through the air and roll no more than 5 percent of the distance. I need backspin to stop the ball before it goes off the straight and narrow.

To sum up, the swing for inside 30 yards is unlike any other swing except the putting stroke because you must concentrate on keeping the clubhead square from the moment the downswing begins until the end of the short through stroke. I can turn the clubface slightly on a short-game shot of a longer distance and still land close enough to the flag for a two-putt green. But when I stand only 30 yards from the pin, I tell myself it will be a criminal offense to two-putt when a one-putt green is mine for the making.

TOUCH-AND-FEEL DRILLS

1. Grip a short iron with only your right hand and hit balls for 15 minutes, concentrating on hitting each

one with a square blade; do not be concerned with how far you hit them. Finish by placing a bucket about 10 yards directly in front of you and hitting 10 straight balls so they fly directly over the bucket. Repeat this for 15 minutes, swinging with only the left hand, again making 10 straight balls fly directly over the bucket.

2. Get a child's stool, a milk crate or a large bucket. Sit on the bucket facing a ball. While sitting, swing at the ball with a short iron, making sure you impact the ball with a square blade. Hit balls for 15 minutes and you'll get the feel of using only the shoulders, arms and hands while keeping the clubhead square from takeaway to the through swing.

Sitting on a bucket or stool, swing at a ball, impacting with the blade square. You'll get the feeling of using only shoulders, arms and hands while keeping the clubhead square.

DAY EIGHT

From 20 Yards Out

Now that we are almost eyeball-to-eyeball with the flag, we must modify our strategy and, most likely, our choice of weapons. Up to now we have used the pitching wedge to arc the ball from 90 to 95 percent of the distance to the target, hoping to roll it the remaining 5 to 10 percent. We wanted to keep the ball airborne as long as possible, hoping that the ball's backspin would bring the ball to a stop almost as soon as it hit the ground.

But now we want the ground to help us. We will drop the air–ground ratio to 75 percent airborne, 25 percent on the ground. And the reason for this change is a simple one: From this short distance, we don't want to hit the ball too hard and go over the green.

How can the treacherous ground—with grass that can slow up the ball, or bumps that change its direction—help us? Let's look at this situation from start to finish.

Assume, first of all, that you are on a fairway level with the green. If the green is above or below you, your thinking and choice of weapons will change—as I will explain later in this lesson.

If you're level with the green, however, and only about 20 yards away, you need a much lower trajectory shot than the one from 40, 50 or 100 yards away. From that distance you want to hit a pop fly that comes down at a steep angle and stops quickly on the green. You cannot trust 40, 50 or 100 yards of fairway grass to keep your bounding ball on a straight line.

Now you face only about 20 yards of fairway grass. If you take a pitching wedge and try to loft the ball over those 20 yards to land near the pin, you are attempting a most delicate shot—one you may use only once or twice a round. True, you may plop the ball 3 feet from the flag, but you are much more likely to pinch the ball out of the turf, get too much backspin and land the ball short, or catch too much of the ball and drive it over the green.

Don't take the chance. This shot calls for a nine-iron (or an eight-iron) that has enough loft to get the ball airborne for 75 percent of the distance but that also has the straighter clubface that will produce a lower trajectory—a line drive rather than a pop fly. From here you want to make use of the bounce and run that you can get from the ground. A line-drive shot will also cause the ball to move forward with such speed that it is not likely to be thrown off course by the 25 percent of ground, much of it carpeted green, that it must cover. In short, you know you can utilize the ground because when the ball hits the ground, it will jump forward.

Grip the club down so your fingers are almost touching the metal. The stance is very narrow, your feet and legs almost touching—we want no "send" from the body. I bring up my hands only to between my knees and waist, lower than I would with a wedge since I hold more firepower than I do with a wedge.

Do not cock your wrists as you do for all other

The wrists stay almost parallel with the ground for this line-drive shot. On the through swing the wrists also come up only to a level parallel with the ground. They do not cock as they do for other through swings.

fairway shots. For this line-drive shot, the wrists stay almost parallel with the ground. As a result, you bring down the nine- or eight-iron with a descending blow that traces an arc less steep than you would trace with a wedge.

Result: You impact the ball with a forward motion of the clubhead, taking a shallow and short divot. I bring the clubhead up to between my knees and waist, the ends matching, but my wrists do not cock as they do on other short-iron through swings. The wrists come up only to a level that keeps them parallel with the ground.

What happens, therefore, is that the loft of the nine- or eight-iron and the forward motion of the clubhead get the ball airborne. That same forward motion of the clubhead gives the ball forward action when it lands. The ball will jump forward through the fairway grass and roll across the green's carpet. That forward run will give it the momentum to bounce straight through the fairway grass to the target.

Now let's suppose the green is above or below you. Your choice of weapon could be the pitching wedge or the sand wedge. You want loft on the clubface to shoot the ball as high into the air as possible, making as few bounces as possible when it lands. You don't want the ball to run, especially when you are hitting to a green below you. The downward slope could carry the bouncing ball past the green.

I bring up my hands waist high, the level that my touch-and-feel gauge tells me is right for a wedge from this distance. I cock my wrists because I want a steeply descending blow that will get the pop-fly trajectory I need. I take a lazy, easy swing, concentrating on contacting the bottom of the ball with the clubface's loft. I follow through waist high, my wrists again cocking as they would for a fairway swing.

For most shots from this distance you will be more or less level with the green, and your key thoughts should be that you want to hit the ball with only enough force so that it will go at least to the green. You also want to hit it low enough so that you can use the ground to slow the ball to a stop before it rolls past the cup.

TOUCH-AND-FEEL DRILLS

1. Stand on your left foot and swing at a ball with a short iron. To prevent yourself from toppling or missing the ball, you must swing the club in a slow, almost lazy motion. Hit 15 balls standing on your left foot, another 15 standing on your right. If you topple or whiff a shot, start over until you have made 15 shots in a row. This will help to teach you to keep your body out of the swing and to swing slowly and easily since we are not concerned about distance.

2. To remind your muscle memory when to cock and when not to cock the wrists, bring back a pitching wedge and cock your wrists so that they are almost at a 90-degree angle to the ground. Look back and relate that positioning of the wrists to the feeling you must have with a pitching or sand wedge. Swing at an imaginary ball and cock your wrists upward at almost a 90-degree angle at the end of the through swing. With

Look back to relate the difference in positioning the wrists for a pitching wedge (to get the ball upward quickly) and for an eight- or nine-iron (to send the ball on a line-drive trajectory).

the pitching or sand wedge clubs you must be able to cock your wrists and uncock your wrists during the downswing to produce the sharply descending blow that will get the ball to shoot upward quickly.

Then pick up an eight- or nine-iron and bring it back while keeping your wrists almost parallel to the ground. Your wrists should not break. Next bring the club down and through as you swing at an imaginary ball and see that your wrists stay almost parallel to the ground—they do not cock upward—at the end of the through swing. By not cocking your wrists at both ends of the swing, you'll send the ball on a line-drive trajectory.

For 15 minutes practice not breaking the wrists at both ends of the swing while swinging an eight- or nine-iron at an imaginary ball. For another 15 minutes practice cocking, or breaking, the wrists at both ends while swinging a wedge.

DAY NINE

From Within 10 Yards

As the song says, you can call it a to-may-to and I can call it a to-mah-to, but we are still talking about the same vegetable. Similarly, in golf, you can call it a chip and I can call it a pitch-and-run, but we are talking about the same thing—covering a short distance by sending the ball half the distance through the air and the other half the distance on the ground.

Here's why I prefer to call this shot a pitch-and-run rather than a chip. When golfers think about chipping, they often think they must get the ball up into the air high enough so that it will land close to the pin. Trouble is, of course, that the ball will land too close to the pin and run too far past it, perhaps over the green. I like to call this shot a pitch-*and*-run because it should be a shot that goes half the way through the air *and* half the way on the ground.

Why 50–50 rather than 75–25, the ratio we used to cover 20 or so yards?

Well, first of all, we know we must hit a line-drive shot for the same reason we hit a line drive from 20 yards away—a high trajectory pop fly is much more likely to go over the green. But if we try to make a line drive go 75 percent through the air from this distance, as we did from 20 yards out, we are also likely to hit the ball too far.

The perfect ratio is 50–50, the ball landing halfway to the pin and then rolling the rest of the way, a ratio that reduces considerably our chances of going over the green. If the ball stops short of the pin, that's not ideal, but you are in a much better position than if the ball stops beyond the green. That's because if you end up 5 or 10 yards beyond the green, you face the same shot you just muffed, and you've wasted a stroke.

The seven-iron is the perfect club for the even distribution you need for the pitch-and-run: 50 percent pitch, 50 percent run. If you take the club back the proper distance and bring it forward the proper distance, the clubface will give you the loft to get the ball halfway to the pin. Then your swing arc and speed will give you the forward action to roll the ball the second half of the way.

To execute this shot, stand with your feet very close together, no more than 2 or 3 inches apart. Grip the club down so that your hands may even be touching the metal shaft. Stand close to the ball because you need no body action or weight shift at all; in fact, your weight should already be heavily on the heel of your front foot.

Stroke the ball pretty much as you would putt a ball. On the takeaway, the clubhead just barely lifts off the grass, only a little higher than you would lift the club if you were putting. Just as though you were putting, the blade must stay square to the target line for the entire takeaway. Bring the club forward to the ball square to the target line. Impact the ball with a firm crispness— there should be the loud *click!* that you would hear from a firmly putted ball. Remember, if you bring back the club 2 feet on the takeaway, follow through 2 feet.

Again, just as when you putt, keep your head down as you follow through, giving the ball the "send" it needs to go up into the air and then roll. Think pitch, think run.

Weekenders have great success with this shot because it is so similar to putting, and because they are aiming at a target—the ground in front of them— that may be only 5 to 10 yards away. Too many golfers, however, attempt this shot when they are out of range. Out of range, let me stress, is standing more than 20 yards from the green. Their swing can't control the run portion of the shot—there's just too much run yardage—and the ball ends up short of the green or over it.

I tell weekenders to practice this pitch-and-run shot almost as often as they practice their putting. "Sad to say," I tell them, "there will be days when your short-iron swing is simply not as good as it should be. You will miss greens short or long, or on the left or right. You may not be missing the greens by much—10 yards or so—but there will be days when you miss most or all of them.

"In other words, you might need this shot for every hole. If your pitch-and-run is accurate, it can turn a bad day into a good or even a great day. The pitch-and-run can give you the chance to score a par or a bogey (that's a par for a player who shoots in the 90s). The well-played pitch-and-run will land the ball close enough to the flagstick for the one-putt that makes up for the stroke you lost by missing the green."

TOUCH-AND-FEEL DRILLS

1. Place two markers on the ground, one about 10 yards away from you, the other about 20 yards. Toss a ball underhand so that it lands no more than a foot from the first marker and then rolls to within 3 feet of the second marker. Then, taking a seven-iron, swing at a ball with the same touch and feel that you felt when you tossed the ball underhand. Alternating between tossing balls and hitting balls with the seven-iron, continue this drill until you place five thrown balls in a row and five struck balls in a row within 2 feet of the second marker.

2. Gripping a seven-iron, hit a ball and then stop your swing right after impact, aiming to stop the ball at a marker about 10 yards away. Then swing and follow through, aiming to land the ball near the 10-yard marker so that it then rolls to a second marker 20 yards away. Alternate for a half hour between stopping at impact and following through and you will be giving to your muscle memory the touch and feel of executing the full pitch-and-run shot.

Hitting 140 Yards to a Par-3 Green

There are par-3 holes that stretch 200 yards and longer, but at those distances, we are no longer talking short game. When you must hit a ball more than 140 yards, you are moving into what I call the "oomph" category—the body has got to add muscle to the swing. To hit a par-3 green from 140 yards or less, however, you use the same weapons and the same swing that you would use for a shot from within 100 yards.

There is, however, a difference between hitting a ball 140 yards from a par-3 tee and hitting a ball 140 yards from the fairway.

And I say, *Vive la différence!* You can tee up a ball when you hit from the tee, but the ball may be nestled deep in the grass when you swing from a fairway.

Teeing up the ball gives a golfer a tremendous psychological advantage. He or she is being asked to send the ball through the air, to make it airborne, when in fact the ball, set on a tee, is already in the air! The tee, in a sense, has done the job for you.

Yet I see golfers set their ball on the grass when they stand at a par-3 tee. I say to them, "Whenever the

Hitting the ball off a par-3 tee from grass (left) or from a tee set too high (center) is usually a mistake. Tee **down** the ball (right).

rules allow you to take an advantage in this game, take advantage. That certainly includes teeing up your ball on a par-3 hole, no matter how short it is."

When you tee up a ball on a par-4 or a par-5 hole, you press the tee into the ground so that as much as a quarter of an inch of the tee is visible. You want the ball to sit high so you can sweep it off the tee with a wood.

But on a par-3 hole, you should not tee *up* the ball. You should tee *down* the ball.

You probably already know why. With all irons, even from a tee, you want to impact the ball with a descending blow. Hit down to get up. You aim the steep downswing so the clubhead catches the ball on its bottom.

If the ball is teed up too high, however, the clubhead may come under the ball, clipping the tee while popping the ball up into the air. The ball should be teed so that it is touching the blades of grass. Put another way, the ball should sit about a finger's width above the turf.

Now that the ball is teed *down*, what club should you use? I nearly always choose a club that's one club stronger than I would use for this distance if the ball were sitting on the fairway. If I would use a pitching wedge for a fairway shot, I will go to a nine-iron for a shot from the tee. If I would use a nine-iron from the fairway, I will go to an eight-iron from the tee.

Here's why: Since the ball is already in the air, it will go higher than a ball hit from the turf. And since I will impact the ball at its bottom, it is going to be rotating counterclockwise, meaning the backspin will stop the ball quickly when it lands. I need more firepower to make up in distance what I will lose because of backspin and extra height.

In addition, the stronger club gives me the extra confidence that if I impact the ball properly, I will reach the green. Just as important, if I don't impact the ball perfectly, I know I should at least reach the green. Also, I know that on most par-3 holes, I am better off being long rather than short, since on most holes the hazards are frontal hazards.

For anything more than 100 yards, you need a little more body work in your swing. That means a fuller turn of the shoulders during the takeaway. Be sure that as the shoulders turn, you bring the club *up*, not *around*, the way a baseball slugger brings his bat around as he waits for the pitch. If you bring the club around, you will bring down the club in a shallow arc. For this shot, like any short-iron shot, you need a steeply descending arc that produces a descending blow that impacts the ball and continues downward to cut the surface of the ground.

For a distance more than a hundred yards, you need a fuller turn of the shoulders during the takeaway. But be sure the club comes **up**, not around.

Loosen your grip at the top of a practice backswing so the shaft falls between your neck and shoulders. Do the same at the end of a practice swing to get the feeling of a full finish with the hands above the shoulders.

After impact, the body comes around as it would for any other tee shot, the weight shifting *rapidly* to the front foot after the clubhead clears the front leg. You want to get the body's oomph into the swing more quickly than for shorter shots for the body work (and the "send") that you need.

I think you get the message: You must have "send" for a shot of this distance. So it is extremely important that the through swing match the extent of the takeaway. If you brought your hands *up* and over the shoulders in the takeaway, you must bring the hands *up* and over the shoulders at the finish. In short, no baseball swing below the shoulders on the takeaway, no stopping on the through swing and no hands below the shoulders at the finish. That full finish ensures that the ball has the "send" to reach the green and the straightness to land close to where you want it to land.

TOUCH-AND-FEEL DRILLS

1. As you bring the club up above your shoulders on the takeaway, loosen your grip on the shaft so that the club falls in the notch between your neck and shoulders. Regrip the club and slowly bring it down, through and up above the shoulders in the through swing. Again loosen your grip and let the club drop into the notch between your neck and shoulders. This will give you the touch and feel of making a full backswing and a full finish above your shoulders.

2. Repeat the first drill for Day Five.

Your Short Game When It's Windy or Wet

WHEN IT'S WINDY

When you stand at the tee, or when you face a fairway shot of 200 yards to a green, you must go through that familiar routine we see so often when TV takes us to a tournament. We all copy the Palmers and the Trevinos by pulling up a few blades of grass and tossing them into the air to see which way the wind is blowing. But when you come to within 100 yards of the green, you need to factor the wind into your thinking only when the wind is blowing more than 15 or 20 miles an hour. Let's assume that a strong wind is whipping across the course as you come to within 100 yards.

You Are 60 to 100 Yards Away

From this distance a strong wind is going to blow your ball short or long, or left or right of its flight line. I use a very simple rule: If the wind is blowing into my face, I use the same club I always use for this distance.

But—and this is a big but—if I would bring my hands up to my shoulders in a no-wind situation, here

I bring the hands *above* my shoulders to hit into the wind. I will be making a longer swing arc—and thus gaining more clubhead speed. That fuller swing will make up for the 8 or 9 yards that the wind may cost me.

If the wind is really blowing hard into my face, I will take a stronger club—an eight instead of a nine—and again make that fuller swing to gain the firepower to cover the 15 to 20 yards the wind may take from me.

Similarly, if the wind is blowing toward the green, I again will use the club I would normally use for this distance. But I will make a shorter swing arc—my hands may rise only to my belt instead of to my shoulders—to reduce the swing speed and allow the wind to blow the ball the 8 or 9 yards that the slower swing speed will cost me. Again, if there is a hurricane-like wind blowing from behind me, I will take a weaker club—a nine instead of an eight—and make that shorter swing arc. I'm looking for the shorter swing arc to cancel out the strong tail wind and land the ball on the green instead of 20 yards past the green.

"But suppose the wind is blowing from right to left or left to right, Walter," golfers say to me. "Or suppose I can't tell which way the wind is swirling down there at the green."

My answer is a simple one: "If you can tell which way the wind is blowing—say it's blowing from the left to the right—aim to the left of your target so that the wind will take the ball to the right. But if you can't tell which way the wind is blowing, aim for the widest section of the green so that even if the wind blows the ball left or right, you likely will land on the green. Mission accomplished."

In fact, whenever you play on a windy day, it is an excellent rule of thumb to aim always for the center of the green—and not for the part of the green where the flag is flying. Here's one good reason why: Sometimes when you hit a really strong shot the ball will bore right through a crosswind or a head wind—and the wind will not turn the ball at all. It goes straight. If you've aimed for the center of the green, you'll land on the center of the green—and, again, mission accomplished.

What you can also do on a very windy day from this distance is bounce the ball to the green with a pitch-and-run shot—50 percent through the air on a lower trajectory and 50 percent on the ground. You can't do this, obviously, if the green is guarded by frontal bunkers. However, if there is nothing in your way, take a five- or six-iron, shorten your swing arc while making sure that you impact the ball with the clubface square; you'll get a low trajectory shot that, hopefully, will cover 50 percent of the distance in the air and 50 percent on the ground.

I know I have been telling you that a shot of this distance should be at least 90 percent in the air, but if you can't trust the air because of the wind, then you must trust the ground to be kind to you—at least in this situation.

Our American pros must make this adjustment when they play the British Open. They play close to a 99–1 short game on American courses—the ball is in the air 99 percent of its journey, 1 percent on the ground. No fools, they. The pros know that American greens are watered and combed to a soft lushness. When a ball hits a green, it stops as though it landed on a beach blanket. But at the British Open they must play on seaside links where the wind swirls fiercely. The pros don't want the ball up in that treacherous air too long. They must play more of an on-the-ground game than an in-the-air game. What helps is that the ground on British courses is especially hard because the fairways are not watered as much as we water them here. The pros know the hard ground will give the ball the bounce and roll it needs to cover the last half of the distance to the target.

You Are 30 to 60 Yards Away

The closer you get to the green, the shorter the ball's flight time. To make the flight time even shorter on a windy day, go to a stronger club—an eight-iron instead of a nine-iron—and take a shorter swing arc to reduce the clubhead speed. Hit a low-trajectory pitch-and-run shot that will land about one-third of the way to your target—the green or the pin—and then run the rest of the way. Again, you should be facing no frontal hazards that will catch the ball as it runs.

One reminder: Make sure you impact the ball with the clubface at a right angle to the ground. On this shot some golfers try to close the blade, or "hood" it, to lower the trajectory of the ball's flight. Advanced players get away with this, but most weekenders close only the toe of the blade. Result: a low hook. Trust the straighter clubface to keep the ball low and your touch-and-feel gauge to make a swing arc that will send the ball about 30 percent through the air and 70 percent on the ground to cover the distance to your target.

You Are Within 30 Yards of the Green

From this distance the wind will have no effect on the low pitch-and-run shot you should be using—going 50 percent through the air and 50 percent on the ground. Make your normal pitch-and-run shot.

WHEN IT'S WET

My first rule when playing in the rain or on a fairway made mushy by rain is this: Leave your pitching or sand wedge in your bag. The wedge's thick flange will dig deep into the turf on its downward blow; if it sticks in the mushy turf, the club will come to a stop and not complete its up-and-through arc. You don't want a stabbing swing, you want a flowing swing. Also, the wet turf will grab the clubhead, causing the shaft to twist in your hands.

When hitting from wet or muddy grass, use an eight- or nine-iron. Grip the shaft more firmly than you usually do. The wet grass will grab and hold even the thinner blade of the eight- or nine-iron. Take the club up on a wider arc than the more V-shaped arc you usually trace with a short iron. It's true that you always must bring down the short-iron club with a descending blow, but bring down the clubhead so that it only skims through the turf, making a very shallow divot. That slightly flatter swing arc will give the wet grass less of a chance to slow or stop the clubhead.

When hitting from wet grass, take the club back on a wider arc (as I am doing with the club in my right hand) than the usual V-shaped arc I am tracing with the club in my left hand. You want to skim through the turf on the downswing, making a shallow divot.

Keep this in mind: A ball hit from wet grass will have little backspin. The wet grass, squeezed between the clubhead and the ball, erases the ball's spin. When the ball lands, as the pros say, it's "hot"—it will run as though scalded. These "flyers," as they're also called, can run 20 or 30 yards longer than a ball hit from a dry fairway. It's usually wise to choose a club that's one or two clubs weaker than what you would use for this distance from a dry surface.

When playing under these unusual conditions—the course windy or wet—I tell weekenders that when in doubt, choose your most comfortable club. That's because unusual conditions often call for unusual shots. You may want the ball airborne for a shorter time, perhaps for only 10 percent of the trip, instead of 50 percent for the usual pitch-and-roll.

The "book" might call for a nine-iron, but if you are more comfortable with a six or even a five, shorten your grip and modify your swing arc so that you can do what needs to be done—specifically, to hit the ball straight to your target. If you are much more likely to impact the ball with the clubhead square when swinging your favorite five-iron rather than the nine-iron that the distance calls for, go for it with the five. Unusual conditions often call for unusual tactics. It's always a confidence booster, when you're under pressure, to bring along a friend.

TOUCH-AND-FEEL DRILLS

1. Stand in tall grass and swing a sand wedge six times at an imaginary ball. You will feel the grass

grabbing the club. Then take six swings with a nine-iron. You will feel the thinner cutting edge of the nine-iron shear through the grass. Then take six swings with the sand wedge again, swinging now a little harder and with a fuller follow-through. You will get the feeling that you had with the nine-iron of shearing through wet grass and turf, not allowing anything to slow or stop the swing.

2. Stand in a practice bunker and swing a sand wedge six times at an imaginary ball, digging the club into and through the sand. Then swing a nine-iron six times and you will find that you can clip the club through the sand much more easily, taking a shorter and shallower divot. Keep alternating for a half hour between the two clubs and you will get the sensation with the sand wedge that you have with the nine-iron: one, that you must not allow the clubhead to stop; and, two, that you must keep firm finger pressure on the shaft to keep the clubhead from turning as it goes through wet grass or turf.

Hitting over a Hazard to a Green

Imagine this: I hand you a tennis ball. I stand 3 feet away from you and ask you to throw the ball to me. I would suspect that you would flop your wrist downward, then bring the wrist upward, flipping the ball to me on a steeply rising upward arc.

Now I am standing 50 feet away from you. Again I ask you to throw the ball to me. For this distance, I would guess, you would bring your arm backward like a bowler, your wrist straight, and then as you bring the arm forward, you would release the ball. On your follow-through the wrist would still be straight and almost parallel to the ground, giving you the force you need for a throw of that distance.

I use that example when I teach golfers how to pitch a ball over a nearby hazard such as a tree, a bush, a stream, a mound or a bunker. Just as you would flip the ball to someone 3 feet away, you flip the golf ball over the hazard. And the trick, as with the tennis ball, is all in your wrists.

Let me explain that by showing you how the swing for a fairway shot for distance is very similar to the motion of throwing the ball 50 feet. For a fairway shot, you bring the club up with your arms extended, creating as wide an arc as possible. Because your arms are extended, you don't break or cock your wrists until late in the upswing. Similarly, on the downswing, you uncock, or release, your wrists at the last possible moment, ideally when the clubhead has passed your beltline or thigh.

For the usual fairway swing, late cocking of the wrists.

The formula for the fairway swing is: Late cocking of the wrists plus late release of the wrists equals all the distance the club can produce.

The reverse is true for the flip shot with a short iron over a hazard: Early cocking of the wrists plus early

For the flip shot, early cocking of the wrists.

release of the wrists equals high trajectory and little distance. You want a sharply descending blow that will shoot the ball upward quickly in a steep arc as it floats over the hazard or obstacle between you and the green.

For this swing, therefore, cock the wrists early, as early as when the clubhead passes the right foot. Bring up your hands high, because you want as high a swing arc as the early cocking of the wrists allows. You are going to get height with this swing, but the height will cost you distance. Bring up your hands to the point that your touch-and-feel gauge tells you is the right point for this distance.

As you start down with the club, release your wrists early to produce that steep downswing you need for the ball's steep upward flight. Your wrists should release when the clubhead is above the waist or about waist high.

An important reminder: Keep the body out of the action. Weekenders try incorrectly to scoop the ball to get it up. Instead, let the downward blow and the wedge's or nine-iron's loft do the work of getting the ball up quickly and steeply.

Finally, bring your hands high to a finish that is as high as the height reached by your hands on the takeaway. The through swing is always important, but it is especially important for this shot. You want to give "send" to the ball to get all the distance that you are losing because of the height of the ball's trajectory. If the flag is 40 yards away, you want to get enough send with your swing to cover that distance.

What club do you choose? If you need a lot of height—to clear a tree or a bush—you probably

The club in my right hand is tracing the usual arc of a golf swing, much like the line formed by a wide and deep saucer. The club in my left hand is tracing a line formed by a narrow horseshoe.

should select a sand wedge, the most lofted club in your bag (or an L wedge, which also has a lot of loft). On the other hand, if you must clear a low-lying bunker and then reach a flagstick some 30 yards beyond the bunker, you need less loft and a lot more distance, so you might go with a seven-iron.

The arc of the golf swing is often likened to a line formed by a wide and deep saucer. For this shot, think of the swing as a line formed by a very narrow horseshoe.

TOUCH-AND-FEEL DRILLS

1. Grip a nine-iron with your right hand; bring it back until your wrists cock, then bring down the club by quickly releasing, or uncocking, your wrists, and hit a real or imaginary ball. Follow through with the club to the height you reached on the upswing. Do that for 15 minutes. You will get the feeling of early cocking and uncocking of the wrists.

2. Flip a ball upward so that it comes down on a sheet of newspaper 2 feet away from your feet. Do that a dozen times. Then move the sheet of paper so that it is 30 feet away from you. Toss the ball so that it lands on the paper at least six out of ten times. Then bring back the paper to a point 2 feet away and flip the ball a dozen times in a row so that it lands square on the paper. Flipping the ball 2 feet will give you the feeling of early cocking and uncocking, which you must use for the flip shot over a hazard. Tossing the ball 30 feet will give you the feeling of late cocking and uncocking of the wrists, which you must use for most golf shots.

_____

Hitting from Rough or Trees to a Green

I obey a strict rule when I hit a ball into rough or trees: If the ball is so deep in the rough that I can't see it, I "bail out"—that is, I hit the ball back onto the fairway even if that means going away from the green. I also bail out if the ball's so deep in the trees that I can't see the green.

Put another way, I am giving up one stroke, paying the penalty for hitting the ball to the wrong place, but I am refusing to risk losing two or three strokes trying to hit to a green from a bad lie.

HITTING FROM ROUGH

If I can see the ball in the rough—that is, if it's sitting atop the grass—then I will play the shot as I would play any fairway shot, using whatever club I know is right for this distance.

If I see the ball nestled deep down in tall grass, I need a pitching wedge or a sand wedge. They have the thick flanges that dig deep to where I want the clubhead to land: behind the ball. And they have the high degree of loft to do what I want them to do: slide under the ball and loft it out of the rough.

The big mistake I see weekenders make when hitting out of rough: They think they need a hard swing. They swing so hard they move their body. When that happens, rather than landing behind the ball and catching the bottom of the ball, the clubhead hits the ground behind the ball or catches the middle of the ball. You won't get the ball to move very far this way—if it moves at all.

You do need a fast swing, however—that is, a swing with a lot of clubhead speed. Clubhead speed ensures that the ball goes high and as far as possible out of the rough. To get that clubhead speed, extend your arms on the upswing. You also need to bring up your hands higher on the upswing than your touch-and-feel gauge would indicate for this distance, again because you need clubhead speed to get through the grass that will try to snare and hold the clubhead.

But like all short-game swings, it is a swing that impacts the ball with a sharply descending blow—not as horseshoe-shaped as your swing from wet grass, but more V-shaped than your swing for a fairway shot.

Impact the ball with your weight evenly balanced. After impact the grass will try to hold back your club. Bring the clubhead through that grabbing grass by making sure your hands finish at the same height on the through swing that they reached on the takeaway swing. Match the ends!

Remember this note of caution: A ball hit out of deep grass will "squirt," becoming what the pros call a "flyer." It will run like a rabbit after it lands. That's because grass gets between the clubface and the ball, taking away backspin. When hitting from deep rough, look for a wide area of the fairway that gives you plenty of running room.

Before you swing, it is always a good idea to ask yourself: Where do I want to be hitting from for my next shot? Aim for that spot, but since we seldom land precisely where we want to land, pick a "comfort zone" area where there is no trouble even if you miss your landing area by 20 or 30 yards.

HITTING FROM TREES

Whether you are "bailing out" from trees by pitching the ball back to the fairway or you are aiming for the green (because there is an opening between the trees), you want to hit what we call a "punch shot." To hit a punch shot, you must disobey the fundamental rule for a perfect golf swing: The ends must match up. For the punch shot, the ends can't match up.

That's because you must hit a low line-drive shot that goes under the branches of the trees. You don't want height, so select a club like a four- or a five-iron; its straight face will keep the ball low and also give you a lot of roll when it lands.

Make sure you choke up the club; you should be looking for no more than 40 yards with this shot. The stance is narrow, feet close together. Bring your hands back only about waist high. As with nearly all short-game shots, keep your body out of the action—only your shoulders, arms and hands are moving. (However, there should be a slight movement of the front knee in toward the ball on the upswing, and a slight

Hitting from trees: The stance is narrow, the hands coming back about waist high, with only the hands, arms and shoulders moving.

Impact the ball with the clubhead as straight as it was at address.
Stop follow-through when hands rise no higher than knees.

movement of the rear knee in toward the ball on the downswing.)

Impact the bottom of the ball with the clubhead as straight as it was at address. Since you don't want height, stop the through swing when your hands rise to no higher than your knees. The ends don't match—the only swing in golf in which the through swing is shorter than the takeaway. That cut-off through swing helps to ensure that the ball stays low, no higher than 10 feet off the ground.

TOUCH-AND-FEEL DRILLS

1. Set three tees in the ground, one opposite your rear foot, one in the middle of your feet and the third about 3 inches beyond your front foot. Swing a club so that you knock over the first two tees, but stop short of knocking over the third tee. Do that for 15 minutes. This will give you the feeling of making a cut-off through swing for the punch shot.

2. Place two balls in deep grass, one opposite your front foot and another opposite your back foot. Swing a wedge or a nine-iron so that you hit the first ball and then continue on to impact the second ball. Do that for 15 minutes. This will give your muscle memory the feeling of a complete follow-through when hitting out of rough.

DAY FOURTEEN

Hitting from a Fairway Bunker

Many golfers are surprised when I tell them they can go for the green from a fairway bunker that is 60 yards or less away. In fact, you can go for a green from a fairway bunker when you are as far as 150 yards away, using a middle iron or a lofted wood. But since we are talking short game, let's look at how a short iron can take you from sand to green.

Two key things to keep in mind: (1) If the ball is half-buried by sand or the bunker has a high bank, it is probably wiser to go by the safest route to the fairway and forget the green; (2) a ball hit out of sand will go only half the distance or less than a ball hit from grass with the same club and the same swing arc.

Let me explain why you lose distance from sand. You must hit down to get the ball up, as we know. When you hit from a bunker, the arc of that descending blow carries the clubhead into the sand, making a divot. And while a grass divot slows down a clubhead to some degree, sand can stop the clubhead dead. That's bad news. There will be a weak follow-through, costing you distance and accuracy.

Therefore, in executing this shot, you need extra

Especially important when hitting out of sand: The body must stay out of the action.

oomph on the downswing to whish the club through
the sand after impact. That doesn't mean you swing
harder by coiling your body on the backswing and
shifting your weight forward just before impact, as you
would for a long shot from the fairway. Just as for
nearly all short-iron swings, the body must stay out of
the action. This is especially important when hitting
from sand. Standing on slippery sand, you are more
likely to sway when you shift your weight. Swaying
throws the clubhead off its swing path. The clubhead
will not land where you are aiming: at the bottom of
the ball. You want a clean, crisp hit that will not catch
sand in front of the ball (causing a droopy shot), and
will not catch the ball at its equator (causing a line-
drive shot that may go straight into the bunker's
bank).

How do you get extra oomph into the swing so that
the clubhead flies through the sand after impact? First
of all, choose a club at least one club stronger than the
one you would choose for a fairway shot—a nine
instead of a pitching wedge, for example. (A sand
wedge is out of the question for a shot of more than 20
yards.) Second, you get extra clubhead speed by
bringing your hands up higher on the upswing than
they would rise for a fairway shot. The longer swing
arc will build greater clubhead speed. The faster the
clubhead is moving at impact, the faster it will go
through the sand after impact.

What I also do on this shot is align my hands a little
forward of the ball at address, instead of their being
aligned with the ball. That ensures that I strike the ball
with a very steeply angled downward blow. The

Align the hands a little forward of the ball at address. That will ensure a steeply angled downward blow.

steeper the swing arc, the higher the ball will rise out of the bunker.

But you also need distance to reach the green. You get the distance by choosing a stronger club and by bringing your hands and clubhead higher than you would for a fairway shot of this distance with this club. Bring down the clubhead in a forceful way *without moving the upper body.*

At impact you have done only half the job of getting the ball to the green. Don't leave the job half done by quitting on the through swing. To give the ball the "send" you need to reach the green—and to overcome the braking action of the sand—you must bring the clubhead up and through by 1) extending the arms to the "shaking hands" position and 2) bringing up the clubhead to the same height you brought it to on the takeaway swing. This shot calls for a sharply descending downswing; but you need a more rounded and full swing arc on the through swing.

One last tip: At address dig your feet deep into the sand. You want a firm foundation because you don't want the body to slip on the sand and move. Don't stand on top of the sand; stand *in* the sand for stability.

TOUCH-AND-FEEL DRILLS

1. Put three tees into the ground: one where you would place the ball for a shot from a bunker, the second about 5 inches away and opposite your front foot, the third about 5 inches in front of that. Swing a

Don't quit on the through swing! Extend the arms, bringing the clubhead up to the same height it reached on the takeaway.

club so that you knock down all three tees. You will be getting the touch and feel of not allowing the clubhead to get stuck in the sand, making it fly through the sand to a high follow-through.

2. Stick a tee into sand at a 45-degree angle. Swing at the tee so that the clubhead hammers the tee into the sand. You will be teaching yourself the hammering-a-nail feeling of using only the shoulders and arms to put oomph into your swing.

Hitting from a Greenside Bunker

It's the saddest sight in golf. You see a player trying to blast a ball out of a greenside bunker. He assumes a perfect stance, feet and legs close together, his body close to the ball. He brings the club back perfectly, cocking his wrists as the clubhead passes his knees. He brings down the club on a steep angle. He impacts the sand 2 inches behind the ball. But he stops the clubhead a split second after impact. The ball flies on a low line, hits the bank of the bunker and rolls back to rest a few inches from where he hit it.

That's sad because up until impact he had done everything perfectly. If he had only brought his hands another 6 to 10 inches higher in the through swing, the ball would have cleared the lip and plopped onto the green.

Paste this into your memory: *It's the follow-through that gets the ball out of a bunker.* It's not the takeaway that gets it out. It's not the downswing that gets it out. It's the through swing that gets it out.

You don't need distance for this shot. The green may be only 10 to 20 feet away from where you stand. And remember, your first goal is to get the ball out; your second goal is to land it on the green; and your third is to land it close to the flag. But your first thought is to get the ball *out.*

Most weekenders are afraid of sand, fearful of being embarrassed like that golfer I just mentioned. I tell those golfers: "Go stand in a bunker and lob a ball underhand onto the green—anywhere onto the green."

They toss the ball underhand with a slow-motion, easy-does-it flipping of the wrists.

"You can do that all day and never once miss the green," I tell them. "Now use that same slow, easy-does-it flipping motion of the wrists, but this time do it with a sand wedge in your hands, using the clubface to 'throw' both ball and sand out of the bunker. You'll soon find out why the pros call the greenside bunker shot the easiest shot in golf."

You are only trying, remember, to blast both ball and sand out of the bunker. You don't need distance; you need only height. Luckily, you are swinging a club that will give you height: The sand wedge is the most lofted club in your bag.

Obviously you don't want the ball to zoom out of the bunker and fly across the green, perhaps landing in another bunker. You want a nice, lazy, soft touch to your swing that lobs the ball onto the grass just the way you would lob it with an underhand toss.

Dig your feet firmly into the sand. Your feet must not slip, which would throw the clubhead out of its proper arc. Your feet and legs are close together, your feet close to the ball. This is strictly an arms-and-hands action. Aim in the direction of the pin. Cock your wrists almost immediately, no later than when the clubhead passes your knees. Your hands go as high as

If the bank of the bunker is very high, the hands should go above the height they reached on the backswing—if possible, above the level of the bunker.

your touch-and-feel gauge tells you to bring them up when you are swinging a sand wedge out of sand. Again, a reminder: You want height, not distance, so your touch-and-feel gauge for the sand wedge should tell you how high the ball will rise when you bring your hands up to, say, shoulder level.

Club speed on the downswing is not a big factor, again because we are not concerned about distance. It is a slow, almost lazy swing. Bring down the club with a force that is the same force you would use if you were tossing the ball underhand onto the green. That is not a lot of force; it is just forceful enough to move the sand and the ball together on what you could call a "carpet of sand." You must impact the sand about an inch to 2 inches behind the ball (the more sand you move, the shorter distance the ball will go).

Now—and underline this—you must follow through, follow through, *follow through.* Bring up your hands and continue through the horseshoe-shaped swing arc. Your hands must rise at least to the level they reached on the backswing.

This swing can be another exception to the rule about the ends matching up. If the bank of the bunker is very high, the hands and the clubhead should go above the height they reached on the backswing— rising, if it's possible, above the level of the bank of the bunker.

TOUCH-AND-FEEL DRILLS

1. Stand in a bunker and toss a ball underhand to a certain spot on the green. Concentrate on tossing the ball using only your hand and shoulder—not your

body. Concentrate on getting the ball up so high that it lands softly near the target with little roll. You will be getting the feeling for the rate of speed that you should swing a club, and the feeling for the force you need to swing a club. Do that for 10 minutes. Then swing a sand wedge at balls for 10 minutes, relating the feeling of the degree of force and the clubhead speed to tossing the ball to the green. Finally, for another 10 minutes, go back to tossing the ball onto the green, again concentrating on relating the feeling of tossing a ball to a green to hitting a ball to a green.

2. Hold a club and swing at an imaginary ball while standing on only one foot in sand or grass. Take a backswing, swing at the ground, then follow through, matching the ends. Do that for 10 minutes, then switch to standing on the other foot and swinging for another 10 minutes. You will be ingraining the feeling of swinging slowly, since you'll fall over if you swing fast. This drill will also teach you the feeling of keeping body action, such as weight shift, out of the swing (shift your weight while standing on one foot and you will also fall down).

Let's Go to the Course!

When you are standing at most tees, you are not thinking about the green because you probably can't even see it. As you come closer—within a long- or medium-iron shot—you think of the green only as flat and square. Land anywhere on the green and you are happy. When you come within 100 yards, you are thinking of quartering the green—that is, aiming for the quarter of the green where the flag is flying. As you come within 50 yards, however, you need to be very aware of the green's dimension and character—round, kidney-shaped, elevated, two-tiered, long and narrow, wide and short, and so on. As you come even closer, you also will see some of a green's particular horrors.

The two most common horrors are the elevated green and the two-tiered green. Let's see how your new touch-and-feel swing can take the horror out of those greens.

THE ELEVATED GREEN

Obviously you want a club that will get the ball up—very much up. You are not concerned about distance from within 50 yards, but you need a club that gives you a lot of height. It could be the sand wedge, the pitching wedge or the newer L-shaped 60-degree wedge—all clubs that shoot the ball up high.

Since the green is elevated, you may be standing on an upslope. If you had to hit the ball 150 yards, the slope would present a problem, since you would need to align your body with the slope. But for a shot of this distance, you don't want body action, so an uphill or downhill lie does not require a change in your stance: feet and knees close together, body close to the ball because you are gripping a very short club.

Keep three things in mind:

First, since you need height, you must bring the backswing *up* rather than taking the wider backswing you would need for a shot of this distance. The swing arc is the same horseshoe-shaped arc you take for hitting out of sand, since you want the ball to get up quickly and get up high. If you make a wide-extension backswing, you will make a wide through swing. The ball will rise too slowly, strike the slope and stop as surely as if it had hit a wall.

Second, you need to strike the ball with a steeply angled downward blow. The steeper the downward blow, the steeper will be the ball's upward flight.

Third, you need to finish with your hands and club rising as high as they did on the takeaway.

I tell weekenders to think about flipping the club when they make this shot. Let's imagine that you are tossing a ball to this elevated green. Since the green is up the hill, you would probably flip the ball underhand to get height as well as distance. Now, with a club in your hands, you need the same kind of flipping

Flip the club up with the wrists at the start of the upswing . . .

... flip down at the start of the downswing ...

... flip up again for the through swing.

action, flipping the hands and arms more than you would for any other golf swing. I flip the club with my wrists at the start of the upswing. I flip it again at the start of the downswing. I flip it up again for the through swing.

Having used the word "flip," I want to make clear that you shouldn't try to pick the ball off the grass or scoop it to the green. When golfers try to scoop or pick, they shift their bodies forward and impact the ball with an upward blow, blading the ball at its equator. What happens, usually, is a ground-ball kind of shot that won't go very far bouncing uphill.

This is a short-game shot that is the same as any other short-game shot, except that the angle that you bring up the club is steeper than the angle for any other shot except one from a bunker. That sharp upswing dictates a steeply angled downward blow that catches the bottom of the ball and quickly sends it upward. The clubhead creates backspin and then makes its divot. The hands and club then come up at the same steep angle and to the same height as the upswing. If your touch-and-feel gauge is as good as it should be at this stage, you are bringing your hands as high as they should rise on the upswing and the through swing.

One last reminder: Since you are hitting uphill, it could be a disaster if you land the ball short of the green. The ball could roll right back to you. If you have any doubts about the club covering the distance because of the yardage you will lose to height, choose a stronger club by one—a nine-iron instead of a pitching wedge, for example. Afraid you'll hit over the green? Remember that you are nearly always in a better position for your next shot when you land beyond the green rather than in front, where you will usually find more bunkers.

THE TWO-TIERED GREEN

As I said at the beginning of today's lesson, if you are 100 or more yards away from this green or any other green, think of the green as flat and square and be happy to land anywhere on it. But if you stand within 50 yards you should be aiming for that portion of the green that will give you the best chance to one-putt.

Obviously, when aiming at a two-tier pin, you hope to land on the tier or level where the pin is cut. Land on the wrong tier and you face a very difficult uphill putt or a downhill putt that is almost as difficult. But since the putt down the hill will leave you on the same level as the pin—while the putt up the hill may roll right back at you if you tap it too softly—you are usually better off landing on a tier above the pin rather than on a tier below it.

A shot to a two-tiered green where the flag is on the lower tier is not as demanding as a shot to a pin on the upper tier. Even if the lower tier is above or below you, you can pitch the ball to the green as you would pitch to an elevated green. Or, if there are no frontal hazards, you can pitch and run the ball as you would to a green level with you.

You must be concerned only about the degree of swing, since the last thing you want to do is to hit the ball so forcefully that it lands on the upper tier. With this club and for this distance, do you take the hands back waist high? Or do you take them back shoulder high or somewhere in between? You will know the answer if you have practiced the drills I have given you so that you know your touch-and-feel gauge as well as you know your telephone number. Then you can check the distance and your club and know how high the hands must go at both ends of the swing.

One other tip on hitting to a lower tier: This is one of the few places on a course where it's better to be short than long. If you land a little short, the ball's forward motion will run it to the green. To avoid that dreaded upper tier, in fact, you might be wise to aim to stop short of the green and then pitch and run it to the pin.

The whole picture changes for the worse when the pin is set on the upper tier. Here you cannot be short. You'll be looking at that very demanding putt up a steep hill. Now it is much better to be long rather than short, even if you must pitch and run another shot from the back of the green. The pitch-and-run shouldn't be as tough as an uphill putt.

Here's my advice: Forget about trying to pitch a ball so that it lands on that hill, which will look like a pinpoint as you stand over the ball. Take a stronger club than you normally use for the distance—a nine instead of a wedge—and take a fuller swing arc than you would normally take for this distance. Then use the ground and play pitch-and-run.

Depending on how far you are from the flag, you can send the ball through the air for about half the distance, more or less, and on the ground the rest of the way up the hill. By now, if you have been practicing your pitch-and-run, you should know how high a swing arc you need to make the ball land where you want and how much clubhead speed you need to make the ball scoot over the grass to the pin.

Forget about the pros you see on television who pitch to an upper-tiered green like this one. Instead play your own game within your own limitations. Use your own skills—don't attempt to borrow the skills of someone else—to get onto the green with as little risk to your score as possible. The bounding pitch-and-run may not be as pretty as the arching pitch shot that hits the green and squiggles to a stop inches from the pin, but it sure is safer.

I'll sum up this lesson and all the other fifteen lessons by saying that your touch-and-feel gauge is going to make your short game a much more accurate game. While that gauge will help you to develop proper swing technique for all the parts of your game, what you must also do before any shot is think. Thinking will turn a fun game into a fantastic game.

About the Authors

Walter Ostroske has been a PGA teaching pro for the past 25 years. He has played in numerous tournaments and has written magazine articles on golf instruction. Currently head pro at the Hempstead Golf and Country Club on Long Island, he is a member of the MacGregor Advisory Staff.

John Devaney is the author of more than 25 books and has written hundreds of magazine articles on sports. The former editor of *Sport Magazine*, he is the editor of Harris Publications golf magazines and is an adjunct lecturer at Fordham University.

Walter Ostroske and John Devaney are the authors of the highly successful *Break 100 in 21 Days: A How-to Guide for the Weekend Golfer, Correct the 10 Most Common Golf Problems in 10 Days* and *Two-Putt Greens in 18 Days: A How-to Guide for the Weekend Golfer.*

ABOUT THE PHOTOGRAPHER

Aime J. LaMontagne is a successful free-lance photographer living in Palmer, Massachusetts. His golfing photographs have appeared in national magazines.

Left to right: John Devaney, Walter Ostroske, Aime LaMontagne

Develop Your Golf Skills with Perigee's How-to Guides for the Weekend Golfer

Break 100 in 21 Days
by Walter Ostroske and John Devaney
For men and women golfers who play mostly on weekends, here's a superfast, easy-to-follow program for shooting in the 80s and 90s, which can be mastered in just 21 days.

Correct the 10 Most Common Golf Problems in 10 Days
by Walter Ostroske and John Devaney
The first book to pinpoint and correct the 10 most common golf problems that hinder a golfer's swing—all in just 10 days!

Power Swing in 15 Days
by Walter Ostroske and John Devaney
Following golf pro Walter Ostroske's instructions, golfers will rid their game of weak shots forever—all in just 15 days!

Shave 10 Strokes in 12 Days
A Woman Golfer's Guide to a More Successful Game
by Sandy LaBauve and George Kehoe
For every woman who has more desire than time to improve her golf game, PGA teaching pro Sandy LaBauve has the answer: a simple, step-by-step 12-day program that covers everything from the grip to putting, chipping, and pitching.

Two-Putt Greens in 18 Days
by Walter Ostroske and John Devaney
This guide offers an easy-to-use daily program that can be completed in 18 days, erasing forever the three-putt greens from your game.

These books are available at your bookstore or wherever books are sold, or, for your convenience, we'll send them directly to you. Call 1-800-631-8571 (press 1 for inquiries and orders), or fill out the coupon below and send it to:

The Putnam Publishing Group
390 Murray Hill Parkway, Dept. B
East Rutherford, NJ 07073

—— Break 100 in 21 Days	399-51600-X	$8.95
—— Correct the 10 Most Common Golf Problems in 10 Days	399-51656-5	$8.95
—— Power Swing in 15 Days	399-51797-9	$8.95
—— Shave 10 Strokes in 12 Days	399-51860-6	$9.95
—— Two-Putt Greens in 18 Days	399-51747-2	$8.95

Subtotal $_____

Postage and Handling* $_____

Sales Tax (CA, NJ, NY, PA) $_____

Total Amount Due $_____

Payable in U.S. funds (no cash orders accepted). $15.00 minimum for credit card orders.
*Postage and handling: $2.50 for 1 book, $.75 for each additional book up to a maximum of $6.25.

Enclosed is my ☐ check ☐ money order
Please charge my ☐ Visa ☐ MasterCard ☐ American Express

Card # _____ Expiration Date _____

Signature as on charge card _____

Name _____

Address _____

City _____ State _____ Zip _____

Please allow six weeks for delivery. Prices subject to change without notice.

Refer to code #65